dreams
do come
true
if only we wish
hard enough

THE MOMENT
YOU DOUBT WHETHER
YOU CAN FLY, YOU CEASE
FOR EVER TO BE
ABLE TO DO IT.

NEVER SAY GOODBYE
BECAUSE GOODBYE MEANS GOING AWAY AND GOING AWAY
MEANS FORGETTING.

IT DOESN'T MATTER IF YOU'RE BORN IN A DUCK YARD,
SO LONG AS YOU ARE HATCHED FROM A SWAN'S EGG

DEEP DOWN, EVERYBODY'S
BEAUTIFUL? - NO.
EVERYBODY'S UGLY.

Talk not
to me of blasphemy, man;
I'd strike the sun
if it insulted me

NEVER STAND BEGGING
FOR THAT WHICH YOU
HAVE THE POWER TO EARN

THERE IS
NOTHING NEW
UNDER THE SUN
IT HAS ALL BEEN
DONE BEFORE

AS SOON AS YOU TRUST YOURSELF,
YOU WILL KNOW HOW TO LIVE.

RESPECT WAS INVENTED TO COVER THE EMPTY PLACE WHERE LOVE SHOULD BE

ALL HAPPY FAMILIES ARE ALIKE, EACH UNHAPPY FAMILY IS UNHAPPY IN IT'S OWN WAY

IF YOU LOOK FOR PERFECTION YOU'LL NEVER BE CONTENT

WOULD IT BE POSSIBLE TO FIND A MORE UNGRATEFUL BOY OR ONE WITH LESS HEART THAN I HAVE! IF ONLY **SUGAR** WERE MEDICINE! I SHOULD TAKE IT EVERY DAY

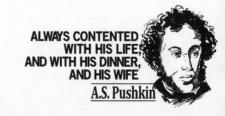

ALWAYS CONTENTED
WITH HIS LIFE,
AND WITH HIS DINNER,
AND HIS WIFE

A.S. Pushkin

F.M. Dostoevsky

POWER IS GIVEN
ONLY TO THOSE
WHO DARE TO LOWER
THEMSELFS AND
PICK IT UP

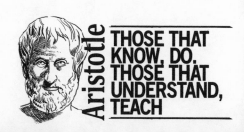

Aristotle

THOSE THAT KNOW, DO. THOSE THAT UNDERSTAND, TEACH

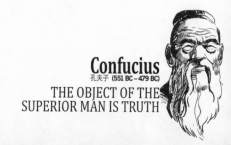

Confucius
孔夫子 (551 BC – 479 BC)
THE OBJECT OF THE
SUPERIOR MAN IS TRUTH

dreams
do come
true
if only we wish
hard enough

THE MOMENT
YOU DOUBT WHETHER
YOU CAN FLY, YOU CEASE
FOR EVER TO BE
ABLE TO DO IT.

"EVER SAY GOODBYE
BECAUSE GOODBYE MEANS GOING AWAY AND GOING AWAY
MEANS FORGETTING."

IT DOESN'T MATTER IF YOU'RE BORN IN A DUCK YARD,
SO LONG AS YOU ARE HATCHED FROM A SWAN'S EGG.

DEEP DOWN, EVERYBODY'S
BEAUTIFUL? NO.
EVERYBODY'S UGLY.

IF YOU KEEP ON BELIEVING, THE DREAMS THAT YOU WISH WILL COME TRUE

HE LOVES ME BECAUSE I'M ME

Talk not to me of blasphemy, man; I'd strike the sun if it insulted me

NEVER STAND BEGGING
FOR THAT WHICH YOU
HAVE THE POWER TO EARN

THERE IS NOTHING NEW UNDER THE SUN. IT HAS ALL BEEN DONE BEFORE.

AS SOON AS YOU TRUST YOURSELF,
YOU WILL KNOW HOW TO LIVE.

RESPECT WAS INVENTED TO COVER THE EMPTY PLACE WHERE LOVE SHOULD BE

WHERE LOVE SHOULD BE

ALL HAPPY FAMILIES ARE ALIKE, EACH UNHAPPY FAMILY IS UNHAPPY IN IT'S OWN WAY

IF YOU LOOK FOR PERFECTION
YOU'LL NEVER BE CONTENT

BREVITY IS THE SOUL OF WIT

GIVE THY THOUGHTS NO TONGUE.

CONSCIENCE DOTH MAKE COWARDS OF US ALL

WOULD IT BE POSSIBLE TO FIND A MORE UNGRATEFUL BOY, OR ONE WITH LESS HEART THAN I HAVE! IF ONLY **SUGAR** WERE MEDICINE! I SHOULD TAKE IT EVERY DAY

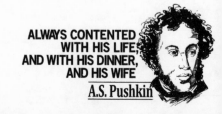

ALWAYS CONTENTED
WITH HIS LIFE,
AND WITH HIS DINNER,
AND HIS WIFE

A.S. Pushkin

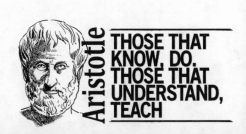

Aristotle

**THOSE THAT
KNOW, DO.
THOSE THAT
UNDERSTAND,
TEACH**

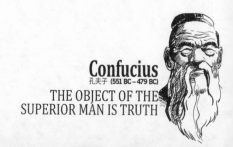

Confucius
孔夫子 (551 BC – 479 BC)
THE OBJECT OF THE
SUPERIOR MAN IS TRUTH

dreams do come **true** if only we wish **hard enough**

THE MOMENT YOU DOUBT WHETHER YOU CAN FLY YOU CEASE FOR EVER TO BE ABLE TO DO IT.

NEVER SAY GOODBYE BECAUSE GOODBYE MEANS GOING AWAY AND GOING AWAY MEANS FORGETTING.

IT DOESN'T MATTER IF YOU'RE BORN IN A DUCK YARD,
SO LONG AS YOU ARE HATCHED FROM A SWAN'S EGG

DEEP DOWN, EVERYBODY'S
BEAUTIFUL? – NO.
EVERYBODY'S UGLY.

Talk not
to me of blasphemy, man;
I'd strike the sun
if it insulted me

NEVER STAND BEGGING
FOR THAT WHICH YOU
HAVE THE POWER TO EARN

THERE IS
NOTHING NEW
UNDER THE SUN
IT HAS ALL BEEN
DONE BEFORE

AS SOON AS YOU TRUST YOURSELF,
YOU WILL KNOW HOW TO LIVE.

RESPECT WAS INVENTED TO COVER THE EMPTY PLACE WHERE LOVE SHOULD BE

LOVE

ALL HAPPY FAMILIES ARE ALIKE; EACH UNHAPPY FAMILY IS UNHAPPY IN IT'S OWN WAY

IF YOU LOOK FOR PERFECTION, YOU'LL NEVER BE CONTENT

WOULD IT BE POSSIBLE TO FIND A MORE UNGRATEFUL BOY OR ONE WITH LESS HEART THAN I HAVE! IF ONLY **SUGAR** WERE MEDICINE! I SHOULD TAKE IT EVERY DAY

ALWAYS CONTENTED
WITH HIS LIFE,
AND WITH HIS DINNER,
AND HIS WIFE

A.S. Pushkin

Aristotle

THOSE THAT
KNOW, DO.
THOSE THAT
UNDERSTAND,
TEACH

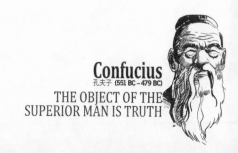

Confucius
孔夫子 (551 BC – 479 BC)
THE OBJECT OF THE
SUPERIOR MAN IS TRUTH

dreams
do come
true
if only we wish
hard enough

THE MOMENT
YOU DOUBT WHETHER
YOU CAN FLY, YOU CEASE
FOR EVER TO BE
ABLE TO DO IT.

NEVER SAY GOODBYE
BECAUSE GOODBYE MEANS GOING AWAY AND GOING AWAY
MEANS FORGETTING.

IT DOESN'T MATTER IF YOU'RE BORN IN A DUCK YARD, SO LONG AS YOU ARE HATCHED FROM A SWAN'S EGG

DEEP DOWN, EVERYBODY'S...
BEAUTIFUL? - NO.
EVERYBODY'S UGLY.

HE LOVES ME
BECAUSE I'M ME

IF YOU KEEP
ON BELIEVING,
THE DREAMS THAT YOU WISH
WILL COME TRUE

Talk not to me of blasphemy, man; **I'd strike the sun** if it insulted me

A MAN IS ALL TIMES... THE BRASS OF HIS WIND

NEVER STAND BEGGING
FOR THAT WHICH YOU
HAVE THE POWER TO EARN

THERE IS
NOTHING NEW
UNDER THE SUN
IT HAS ALL BEEN
DONE BEFORE

AS SOON AS YOU TRUST YOURSELF,
YOU WILL KNOW HOW TO LIVE.

RESPECT WAS INVENTED TO COVER THE EMPTY PLACE WHERE LOVE SHOULD BE

ALL HAPPY FAMILIES ARE ALIKE; EACH UNHAPPY FAMILY IS UNHAPPY IN IT'S OWN WAY

IF YOU LOOK FOR PERFECTION YOU'LL NEVER BE CONTENT

WOULD IT
BE POSSIBLE TO FIND A
MORE UNGRATEFUL BOY
(OR ONE WITH LESS
HEART THAN I
HAVE)

IF ONLY **SUGAR** WERE MEDICINE! I SHOULD TAKE IT EVERY DAY

ALWAYS CONTENTED
WITH HIS LIFE,
AND WITH HIS DINNER,
AND HIS WIFE

A.S. Pushkin

Aristotle

THOSE THAT
KNOW, DO.
THOSE THAT
UNDERSTAND,
TEACH

Confucius 孔夫子 (551 BC – 479 BC)

THE OBJECT OF THE
SUPERIOR MAN IS TRUTH

dreams
do come
true
if only we wish
hard enough

THE MOMENT
YOU DOUBT WHETHER
YOU CAN FLY, YOU CEASE
FOR EVER TO BE
ABLE TO DO IT.

NEVER SAY GOODBYE
BECAUSE GOODBYE MEANS GOING AWAY AND GOING AWAY
MEANS FORGETTING.

IT DOESN'T MATTER IF YOU'RE BORN IN A DUCK YARD,
SO LONG AS YOU ARE HATCHED FROM A SWAN'S EGG.

DEEP DOWN, EVERYBODY'S...
BEAUTIFUL? - NO.
EVERYBODY'S UGLY.

IF YOU KEEP ON BELIEVING, THE DREAMS THAT YOU WISH WILL COME TRUE

HE LOVES ME BECAUSE I'M ME

Talk not to me of blasphemy, man; I'd strike the sun if it insulted me

NEVER STAND BEGGING
FOR THAT WHICH YOU
HAVE THE POWER TO EARN

THERE IS
NOTHING NEW
UNDER THE SUN
IT HAS ALL BEEN
DONE BEFORE

AS SOON AS YOU TRUST YOURSELF,
YOU WILL KNOW HOW TO LIVE.

RESPECT WAS INVENTED TO COVER THE EMPTY PLACE WHERE LOVE SHOULD BE

IF YOU LOOK FOR PERFECTION, YOU'LL NEVER BE CONTENT

ALL HAPPY FAMILIES ARE ALIKE; EACH UNHAPPY FAMILY IS UNHAPPY IN IT'S OWN WAY

WOULD IT BE POSSIBLE TO FIND A MORE UNGRATEFUL BOY, OR ONE WITH LESS HEART THAN I HAVE?

IF ONLY **SUGAR** WERE MEDICINE! I SHOULD TAKE IT EVERY DAY

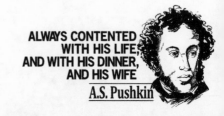

ALWAYS CONTENTED
WITH HIS LIFE,
AND WITH HIS DINNER,
AND HIS WIFE

A.S. Pushkin

F.M. Dostoevsky

POWER IS GIVEN
ONLY TO THOSE
WHO DARE TO LOWER
THEMSELFS AND
PICK IT UP

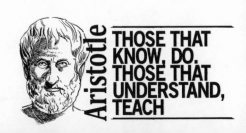

Aristotle

**THOSE THAT
KNOW, DO.
THOSE THAT
UNDERSTAND,
TEACH**

Confucius 孔夫子 (551 BC – 479 BC)

THE OBJECT OF THE
SUPERIOR MAN IS TRUTH

dreams
do come
true
if only we wish
hard enough

THE MOMENT
YOU DOUBT WHETHER
YOU CAN FLY, YOU CEASE
FOR EVER TO BE
ABLE TO DO IT.

NEVER SAY GOODBYE
BECAUSE GOODBYE MEANS GOING AWAY AND GOING AWAY
MEANS FORGETTING.

IT DOESN'T MATTER IF YOU'RE BORN IN A DUCK YARD, SO LONG AS YOU ARE HATCHED FROM A SWAN'S EGG

DEEP DOWN, EVERYBODY'S BEAUTIFUL? - NO, EVERYBODY'S UGLY

IF YOU KEEP
ON BELIEVING,
THE DREAMS THAT YOU WISH
WILL COME TRUE

HE LOVES ME
BECAUSE I'M ME

Talk not
to me of blasphemy, man;
I'd strike the sun
if it insulted me

NEVER STAND BEGGING
FOR THAT WHICH YOU
HAVE THE POWER TO EARN

THERE IS
NOTHING NEW
UNDER THE SUN
IT HAS ALL BEEN
DONE BEFORE

AS SOON AS YOU TRUST YOURSELF,
YOU WILL KNOW HOW TO LIVE.

RESPECT WAS INVENTED TO COVER THE EMPTY PLACE WHERE LOVE SHOULD BE

IF YOU LOOK FOR PERFECTION, YOU'LL NEVER BE CONTENT

ALL HAPPY FAMILIES ARE ALIKE; EACH UNHAPPY FAMILY IS UNHAPPY IN IT'S OWN WAY

WOULD IT BE POSSIBLE TO FIND A MORE UNGRATEFUL BOY OR ONE WITH LESS HEART THAN I HAVE!

IF ONLY SUGAR WERE MEDICINE! I SHOULD TAKE IT EVERY DAY

ALWAYS CONTENTED
WITH HIS LIFE,
AND WITH HIS DINNER,
AND HIS WIFE
A.S. Pushkin

F.M. Dostoevsky

POWER IS GIVEN
ONLY TO THOSE
WHO DARE TO LOWER
THEMSELFS AND
PICK IT UP

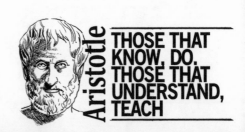

Aristotle

THOSE THAT
KNOW, DO.
THOSE THAT
UNDERSTAND,
TEACH

Confucius
孔夫子 (551 BC – 479 BC)
THE OBJECT OF THE
SUPERIOR MAN IS TRUTH

LOVE LOOKS NO
WITH THE EYES
BUT WITH THE MIN

CHOOSE
A JOB YOU
LOVE, AND
YOU WILL
NEVER
HAVE TO
WORK
A DAY IN
YOUR LIFE

IT DOES NOT MATTER
HOW SLOWLY YOU GO
AS LONG AS YOU
DO NOT STOP

THE GREATEST HAPPINES

IS TO KNOW THE SOURCE O

I INHAPPINESS

THE OBJECT OF THE SUPERIOR MAN IS TRUTH

ET THE BEAUTY
F WHAT YOU LOVE
E WHAT YOU DO

NECESSITY IS
THE MOTHER
OF INVENTION.
PLATO Πλάτων
424 BC – 348 BC

IS NO
Y BUT
AMBLE
HING FOR

MONEY
LIKE ВОДКА